TheBlackPullet

Anonymous

Edition : Culturea (Hérault, 34)
Contact : infos@culturea.fr
Retrouvez notre catalogue sur http://culturea.fr
Imprimé en Allemagne par Books on Demand
Design typographique : Derek Murphy
Layout : Reedsy (https://reedsy.com/)
Dépôt légal : janvier 2023

ISBN : 9791041942794

PREFACE

The work which we offer to the public must not be confused with a collection of reveries and errors to which their authors have tried to give credence by announcing supernatural feats; which the credulous and the ignorant siezed with avidity. We only quote the most respectable authorities and most dignified in faith. The principles which we present are based on the doctrines of the ancients and modern, who full of respect for the Divinity, were always the friends of mankind, endeavoured to recall them to virtue, by showing them vice in all its deformity. We have drawn from the most pure sources, having only in view the love of truth and the desire to enlighten those who desire to discover the secrets of Nature and the marvels which they unfold to those who never separate the darkness which surrounds them. It is only given to those who are favoured by The Great Being, to raise themselves above the terrestial sphere, and to plan a bold flight in the etheric regions; it is for these priviledged men that we write.

To us no importance is given to the splenetic Voices which are raised against us. The silence and the smile of disdain will be the only answer with which We shall oppose them, and we shall follow with firm Sustained steps the route which indicates to us the luminous stars which fill the heavens, which cover our heads, and which light these thousands of worlds, which bless every day with our Sovereign Master of the Universe, which He has created, also ourselves, and whose Will maintains this admirable order, Which commands our admiration, our respect and our love.

The Black Pullet Or The Hen WithTheGoldenEggs

Before beginning the subject, and to acquaint my readers of this profound Science, which until the present day has been the object of research of the most constant and profound meditations, I must unbosom myself how these marvelous secrets were communicated to me, and the manner in which the Divine Providence allowed me to escape from the greatest dangers and, so to speak, conducted me by the Divine Hand, to prove that by Divine Will it is sufficient to raise unto Himself the last of Beings or to precipate to naught those who are clothed with all power on Earth. We all therefor come from God, God is everything, and without God nothing can exist. Who more than I may penetrate the truth eternal and sacred.

I formed part of the expedition to Egypt, an officer in the army of the genius. I took part in the successes and reverses of this army, which victorious or obliged to cede to force from the eventualities and circumstances, always covered itself with glory.

As there is no point in relating here any detail which deals with this memorable campaign, I will but relate one single feature, with which I was touched, and is necessary for the development which I must give to those whom I mentioned in my preface. I had been sent by the General, under whose orders I found myself, to draw up the plans of the Pyramids; he had given me an escort of some mounted light infantry horse. I arrived with them at my destination without experiencing any accident, also without noticing anything that could conjecture the fate that awaited us. We had dismounted near the Pyramids, our horses had been tethered; sitting on the sands we appeased the hunger that tormented us. French gaiety seasoned the food which composed our frugal meal. It was on the point of ending, and I was occupied with my work when all of a sudden a horde of desert Arabs fell on us. We did not have the time to place ourselves in a position of defence. The blows of swords descended upon us, the bullets whistled, and I received several wounds. My unhappy companions were lying on the ground dead or expiring. Our cruel enemies after having removed our weapons and clothes, disappeared with our horses with the speed of lightning. I remained for some time in a state of prostration, facing the sun. At last recovering some of my strength, I raised myself with pain. I had two sword cuts on the head, and one on the left arm. I looked around me. I saw nothing but corpses, a burning sky and arid sand in an immense desert and a frightning solitude. With but the hope of a certain and cruel death, I resigned myself to saying goodbye to my country to my parents and to my friends. Invoking heaven, I crawled to the Pyramid, and the blood which ran with abundance from my wounds reddened the sand which was soon to be my tomb.

Arriving at the foot of these worldly marvels I sat down and leaned against this enormous mass that had seen many centuries pass by and which would see many more pass. I thought that my existence which was soon to end had come to naught just as the day which was nearing its end, the sun being on the point of plunging into the ocean.

"Brilliant star, receive my goodbyes," I said with emotion. "My eyes will never see you again, your benificent light will never shine on me again. Goodbye." As I said this goodbye which I thought was eternal, the sun disappeared. The night came and covered the world with its dark curtain.

I was absorbed with the most sad reflections when a light noise could be heard a few paces from me. A large slab of stone detached itself from the pyramid and fell on the sand; I turned to that side, and by the light of a small lantern that he carried in his hand, I perceived a venerable old man who came out of the pyramid. A white beard covered his chest, a turban covered his head, and the rest of his costume indicated that he was a Mohammedan. He cast his eyes around; then advancing a few steps he halted opposite the corpse of one of my unhappy companions of misfortune.

"Oh Heavens!" he cried in Turkish. "A man is wounded, a Frenchman is dead." He lifted his eyes to the sky saying: "Oh Allah." He then discovered the others which he carefully examined to see if he could not find one who still breathed, and to assure himself, I saw him place his hand in the region of the heart. The old man recognised that they had all ceased to live. Uttering a painful groan, with tears furrowing down from his eyes, he retraced his steps to re—enter the pyramid. I felt the desire to conserve my days. I had already made the sacrifice of my life; hope entered my heart. Summoning all my strength, I called to him; he heard me, and turning his lantern in my direction, he saw me. Advancing he gave me his hand, which I seized and pressed to my ups. He saw that I was wounded and that blood was flowing from the cuts on my head.

Placing his lantern on the ground, he removed his girdle and covered my brow. He then helped me to get up. I had lost a lot of blood and was suffering from extreme weakness—I hardly had the strength to support myself. Placing his lantern in my hand, then taking me in his arms, he carried me near the opening in the pyramid from which he had come and placed me gently on the sand. Giving me an affectionate grip of the hand, he indicated that he was re-entering the pyramid and would return promptly.

I gave thanks to Heaven for the unexpected help that had been sent me. The old man reappeared carrying a flagon. He removed the cork and poured a few drops of the liqueur into a drinking vessel which he gave to me to drink. A delicious perfume diffused around me. Hardly had this Divine Liqueur penetrated my stomach than I felt regenerated, and I had enough strength to enter the pyramid with my benefactor and generous conductor.

We then stopped for a few moments. He replaced the stone that had fallen, which he adjusted with an iron bar, and we descended by an easy slope into the interior of the pyramid. After having walked for some time on the same path, which made several sinuous turns, we arrived at a door which he secretly opened and closed with care. Then having crossed an immense hall, we entered another place. A lamp hung from the ceiling; there was a table covered with books, several oriental divans or seats, and a bed on which to rest. The kind old man conducted me to a seat where he made me sit down. Placing his lantern on the table he opened a kind of cupboard from which he took several vases.

He approached me and invited me to remove my clothes with an attention and complaisance difficult to describe. Having examined my wounds he applied with solemn formality several balms which came from the vases of which I have previously spoken. Hardly had they been applied to my arms and head than the pains were soothed. He invited me to lie on his bed, and very soon a beneficial and soothing sleep weighed down my eyelids.

When I awoke, I looked around and saw sitting near me the good old man who did not wish to partake of rest while I was asleep as he feared that I might need help. I tendered him my most grateful thanks by the most expressive signs. In the same manner he signified to me that I must remain quiet. He gave me a new portion of the cordial which had already proved its happy effects. Afterwards he looked at me with extreme attention, and realizing that he had nothing to fear for my life, he affectionately patted my hand. He then lay down on some cushions on the other side of the chamber where we were, and soon I heard him sleeping profoundly and peacefully.

"Oh benevolent one," I said to myself, "thou art virtue par excellance and a pure emanation of the Divinity; thou unitest and bringest men together and thou makest them forget the pains to which they are prey. Through thee they are returned to happiness, and too thou art this happiness, the object of all their wishes and all their desires."

My host made a movement and got up. He came to me and smiled at seeing me in a state of calm and tranquility which left him in no fear of my being. He gave me to understand that he was going to leave me so that he could go out of the pyramid and see what was happening outside. He brought to my side that which he thought would be necessary for my needs, and then he left me alone.

Until this moment I had not reflected at all on what had happened to me in this exigency. I found myself safe in this subterranean place, and I had no uneasiness relative to my host; however, this would have to come to an end by my departing after I had been cured and re-joining the Army. I was occupied with these ideas when I saw the old man re-enter. He gave me to understand that several Arab corps and Mamelouks were surveying the plain and that he had seen them without being noticed because his retreat was impenetrable to all eyes. He indicated that he had me in his care and regarded me as his son; therefore I could deliver myself to the greatest security. I indicated to him my complete gratitude, and he appeared satisfied.

As I appeared to be dissatisfied to be able to express myself only by signs, he brought me a book indicating that with its help we could soon communicate together without hesitation. The career which I had followed since my childhood had familiarised me with meditation, I loved the application of mind, and I was soon in the condition to listen to my generous old man. He also showed such compliance in the lessons which he gave me that even with less good will, one would have made progress. I remain silent on all that was relative to my new education. My complete cure and convalescence took longer than I realized. My host went out from time to time to see what was taking place as he was in complete ignorance of earthly events.

In short, one day he was longer than usual, and on his return he informed me that the French Army had evacuated Egypt and that I could not hope to leave at this time without giving an account of the days that I had spent with him. I should stay with him which he would make me do by his kindness and love so that in my particular case of captivity my fate would not be as cruel as I might think because he would teach me things which would astonish me and I should desire nothing in the way of good fortune. I had begun to understand the Turkish language. He told me to get up. I obeyed him. He took me by the hand and conducted me to the end of the chamber. He opened a door opposite the one by which one entered, and taking a lamp from the table we entered a vault where there were disposed in regular lines several coffers which he opened. They were full of gold and gems of every kind. "*You* see my son that with this one never fears poverty. Everything is yours; I am reaching the end of my career, and I shall be happy to leave them in your possession. These treasures are not the fruit of avarice and a sordid interest. I own them by the knowledge of Occult Sciences with which I am familiar and the boon which has been granted to me by The Great Being to penetrate the secrets of Nature. I can still command the Powers that populate the Earth and Space and are not visable to ordinary men.

"I like you, my dear son. I recognise in you the candour, sincerity, love of truth, and aptitude for these sciences, and most of all I wish you to know that they have cost me more than eighty years of research, meditation, and experience.

"The science of the Magicians, the language of the hieroglyphics, have been lost by the downfall of man. Only I am the guardian. I will impart these precious confidences to you, and we will read together these characters traced on the pyramids which have been the despair of scholars and before which they have paled for many centuries."

The prophetic manner in which he spoke impressed me and I showed a very lively desire to understand that with which he wished to acquaint me. I told him this in the Turkish language which I was beginning to understand and to talk in a manner so that I could be understood.

"Your wishes shall be fulfilled," answered my adopted father. Then lifting one hand to the arch of heaven, he spoke in a solemn tone: Love, my son, love the very good and the very grand God of the philosophers, and never become proud if he brings you in contact with the children of wisdom for you to associate in their company and to make you a participant in the wonders of his power.

After having finished this invocation of sorts, he then said while looking at me: "Such are the principles which you must fathom. Try and make yourself worthy to receive the light. The hour of your regeneration has come. You will become like a new individual.

"Pray fervidly to Him who alone has the power to create new hearts, to give you that which will make you capable of great things that I have to teach you, and to inspire me to withhold from you none of the mysteries of Nature. Pray. Hope. I eulogise the eternal wisdom which has been placed in my soul and wish to disclose to you its ineffable truths. And you will be lucky, my son, if nature has placed in your soul the resolution that these high mysteries will demand of you. You will learn to command all Nature. God alone will be your master, and the enlightened Will alone be your equal. The supreme intelligences will glory in obeying your desires. The Demons will not dare to be found where you are. Your voice will make them tremble in the pits of the abyss, and all the invisibles who inhabit the four elements will esteem themselves happy to administer to your pleasures. I adore you oh Great God for having enthroned man with so much glory, and having established him as sovereign monarch of all the works made by your hands.

"Do you feel, my son, do you feel this heroic ambition which is the sure stamp of the children of wisdom? Do you dare to desire to serve only the one God and to dominate over all that is not God? Have you understood what it is to prove to be a man and to be unwilling to be a slave since you are born to be a Sovereign? And if you have these noble thoughts, as the signs which I have found on your physiognomy do not permit me to doubt, have you considered maturely whether you have the courage and the strength to renounce all the things which could possibly be an obstacle to attaining the greatness for which you have been born?"

At this point he stopped and regarded me fixedly as if waiting for an answer, or as if he were searching to read my heart.

I asked him, "What is that which I have to renounce?"

"All that is evil in order to occupy yourself only with that which is good. The proneness with which nearly all of us are born to vice rather than to virtue. Those passions which render us slaves to our senses which prevent us from applying ourselves to study, tasting its sweetness, and gathering its fruits. You see, my dear son, that the sacrifice which I demand of you is not painful and is not above your powers; on the contrary, it will make you approach perfection as near as it is possible for man to attain. Do you accept that which I propose?"

"Oh my Father," I answered, "nothing conforms more to my desires that that one should choose propriety and virtue."

"It suffices," answered the old man. "Before unfolding to you completely the doctrine which will initiate you into the mysteries, which are most profound and the most sacred, you must understand that the elements are inhabited by very perfect creatures. The immense space between heaven and earth has inhabitants far more noble than the birds and the gnats. The vast seas have many other hosts than the whales and dolphin. It is the same in the depths of the earth which contains other things than water and minerals, and the element of fire, more noble than the other three, has not been created to abide there useless and empty. The air is full of an unnumbered multitude of beings with human form—a little proud in appearance but in effect docile and great lovers of the sciences; subtle but obliging to the great Mages and enemies of the foolish and the ignorant: these are the sylphs. The seas and rivers are the habitat of the Ondines, the earth is full practically to the center of Gnomes, guardians of the treasures and the precious stones. These are the ingenious friends of man and easy to command. They supply to the children of the Magicians all moneys of which they have need and only ask payment for their services in the glory of being commanded.

"As for the Salamanders, the inhabitants of the fire regions, they serve the philosophers, but they do not seek the attention of their company.

"I could also talk about the familiar spirits: Socrates, as well as Pythagoras and a few other wise men, had his. I have one also; he is near me when I have need of him. This will no doubt seem strange to you, but even if your eyes do not convince you of the truth, you will be able to believe it if you have any confidence in Socrates, Plato, Pythagoras, Zoroaster, Proclus, Porphyry, Iamblichus, Ptolemy, Trismegistus and other wise men to whose enlightenment one must add those who give us the natural knowledge.

"It remains for me to speak to you of the Talismans, those magic circles, which will give you the power to command all the elements, to avoid all the dangers, all the snares of your enemies, and to assure you the success of all your enterprises and the fulfillment of your wishes."

He arose, opened a chest which was at the foot of his bed, and took out a cedarwood box covered in gold veneer and enriched with diamonds of an extraordinary brilliance. The lock on which was engraved hieroglyphic characters was also of gold. He opened this casket, and I saw a large quantity of talismans and rings which were enriched with diamonds and engraved with magical and cabalistic symbols. It was impossible to look at them without being dazzled

"You see, my son, each one has its virtue, its peculiar virtue, but to make use of it you must understand the language of the Magicians in order to pronounce the mysterious words engraved thereon. I will teach them to you before working with you on the great performance with the spirits and the animals who are submissive to my authority and who obey me blindly.

'You will see when you have been initiated into all these mysteries of how many errors the majority of those who pretend to be servile to nature have been guilty. They love the truth and believe they have discovered it by means of abstract ideas and lose their way in the faith of a reason of which they do not know the limits.

"The vulgar or common people do not see over the world in which they live other than an arch of glittering light during the day and a scattering of stars during the night. These are the limited ones of the universe. Certain of the philosophers have seen more and have increased (their knowledge) up to nearly the present time to the point of affrighting our imagination. Further, what prodigious work is offered at one stroke to the human spirit! Employ eternity even to survey it; take the wings of dawn, fly to the planet Saturn in the skies which extend over this planet. You will find without ceasing new spheres, new orbs, worlds accumulating one above another. You will find infinity in matter, in space, in movement, in the number of nuances and shades which adorn them. As our souls expand with our ideas and assimilate in a certain manner the objects which they penetrate, how much then must a man become elated at having penetrated the inconceivable profundities. I am an upstart thanks to wisdom, and you will reach this point too." He arose and took up several manuscripts which were on the table. "These precious books, my dear son, will acquaint you with things unknown to the rest of humanity and which will seem never to have existed. These books escaped the fire of the library of Ptolemy. They have received some damage, as you see; in effect, several pages have been blackened by the fire.

"Ah well! It is by the knowledge which I have been able to draw from these works that I have the authority to command all the beings who inhabit the aerial and terrestrial regions, known and unknown to man.

"Oh my son! Prostrate yourself before the Divinity, deplore in His presence the errors of the human spirit, and promise Him to be as virtuous as it is possible for a man to be. Guard against studying moral philosophy in the ignorant writings of the multitudes, in the schemes produced by the heat of the imagination, by the restlessness of the spirit, or by the desire for celebrity which torments their authors. Seek guidance in those works where, having no other interest than truth or other aim than public usefulness, they render to morals and to virtue the homage which they have deserved in all times and from all peoples."

I listened to this good old man with an admiration mixed with respect; he had stopped speaking and I thought I heard him still. A sweet majesty reigned in all his features, and the persuasion seemed to pour from his lips like a limpid stream running down a slope to fertilize the prairies. He noticed my admiration which was akin to ecstacy.

"My dear son," he said, "I pardon your astonishment. You have until now lived in the society of men who are corrupt, who have learnt to doubt everything and to forget the respect which one owes to Him who has brought forth all from nothing. Wisdom for them a meaningless difficulty, but as you learn it, it will become for you a practical virtue. You will look on it as something very simple, as natural to you as the air you breathe and as necessary to you for your existence. Your wounds are healing. Tomorrow I will commence your education in wisdom, and I will give you the first lesson. I am now going to my aviary to feed my prisoners."

"What!", I said to him. "Your prisoners! With your philosophy and the love of humanity which characterizes you, do you deprive living creatures of their liberty?"

He smiled at my observation. "My dear son, that which I do is necessary to facilitate my mysterious operations, but the destiny of those submissive to my laws is perhaps sweeter than if they enjoyed complete liberty. Besides, they have never known the prize and so cannot desire it. Tomorrow you will have the answer to all these enigmas.

He then left me to enter the cave where he had led me when he showed me the chests filled with gold and precious stones. Soon he came back. I got up. He told me to approach the awning so that we could eat something before going to sleep. He picked up the papers that were on the table. He took a seat and told me to sit by his side. I obeyed, but as I did not see any food, he laughingly added that this food was not very substantial but that in a moment I would see that he had cooks and slaves equally clever and intelligent. He immediately pronounced these words: Ag, Gemenos, Tur, Nicophanta, and blew three times on a ring which he had on his finger. Immediately the place was lit up by seven chandeliers of rock crystal which appeared from the void. Nine slaves entered bringing various viands on golden plates and wine in vessels of the greatest richness. Incense burned in tripods, and celestial music could be heard. Everything was placed on the table in the most beautiful order, and the slaves stood to attention around us to serve.

"You see, my son," the good old man repeated to me, "I have but to command to be obeyed. Eat, serve yourself, and choose what will gratify you."

Everything which I tasted was delicious. Then I took my goblet, and the wine, like nectar, which had been poured into it, its bouquet forefunner to its delicate taste, appealed agreeably to my sense of smell. When it had astonished my pallet and I had relished it, it seemed as though a divine fire flowed through my veins and as if I had acquired a new existence. I looked at the slaves who served us; they were all in the flower of their youth, of the greatest beauty, and dressed in rose silk tunics with white belts. They had flowing golden curls waving on their shoulders. With lowered eyes of respect, they attended to the orders of their master.

The old man allowed me to finish my survey, and he then followed up with: "My son you have appeased your hunger?" "Yes, my Father." He raised his hand and said: Osuam, Bedac, Acgos, and the slaves hurried to remove all that was on the table. They went out, the chandeliers disappeared, and two beds arranged themselves on each side of the apartment which was no longer lit except for the lamp that cast a soft light not unlike twilight.

"There, my dear son, is the manner in which you will be served every day. Your occupations will vary innumerably and thus will preserve you from tediousness. Deliver yourself to sleep, I will do the same, and tomorrow when day appears, I will keep my word which I have given to you."

"But my Father, the daylight will never penetrate into your abode; how can you know when break of day will appear?"

"That depends on my will, my son; it is another surprise that I will arrange for you. Until tomorrow, sleep in peace."

He extended his hand to me, and I pressed it to my heart. He approached his bed, lay down and soon sleep weighed down his eyes. I imitated him for a little while after which I fell asleep.

Then I opened my eyes the lamp had vanished, daylight lit the chamber, and the rays of sun penetrated there. The old man was walking with a book in his hand. The movement that I made interrupted his perusal. He looked at me smilingly. I got up hurriedly and flew into the arms he opened to me.

"My father, I salute you."

"You have rested well, my dear son," he said, as I judge by the calm which reigns on your countenance.

Render homage to God who has permitted you to enjoy again this beautiful day, which lights you, and ere I initiate you into the mysteries of wisdom, I will have a conversation with you on a point of my doctrine which is necessary for developments." He gave me a book and opening it said: "Here is the first page and the prayer which you must address to the Great Being." And I read that which follows:

Oration of the Sages.

Immortal, Eternal, Ineffable, and Sacred Father of all things, who is carried on the chariot rolling without cease, of the worlds which rotate always. Ruler of the Etheric Plain where Your throne of power is exalted and from whose heights Thy formidable eyes discover everything and Your beautiful and saintly ears hear everything. Harken to Your children whom You have loved from their birth through all time. Since Your lasting, great, and eternal majesty shines brightly over the world and the starry heavens, Thou art raised above them. Oh, sparkling fire! There You light and maintain Yourself in the appropriate splendour. There comes forth from Your being never-failing streams of light which nourish Your infinite spirit. This infinite spirit generates all things and makes this inexhaustible treasure of matter which cannot fail to procreate that which always surrounds it because of the forms without number with which it is filled and with which You have filled it since the beginning of time. From this spirit the very saintly kings who are standing around Your throne and who compose Your court also draw their origin. Oh, Universal Father! Oh, Unique One! Oh, Father of blissful mortals and immortals! You have particularly created the powers which are marvelously like Your eternal thought and Your adorable essence. You have established them superior to the angels who announce Your wishes to the world. Finally, You have created us sovereigns over the elements. Our continued exertion is to praise You and to adore Your desires. We burn with the desire to be possessed of You. Oh, Father! Oh, Mother, the most tender of Mothers! Oh, admirable example of tender sentiments of Mothers! Oh, Son, the flower of all Sons! Oh, mould of all our shapes! Well beloved spirit, soul, harmony, and number of all things, we adore You.

When I had finished, he said to me: "My dear son, I have spoken to you of the spirits that populate the firmament, the sea, the earth, and fire, that is to say the elements. I have spoken to you of the spirits and am going to go into greater detail to extend the limits of your intelligence and to give you the means of penetrating into and understanding the sacred mysteries which will be divulged to you.

"When the universe was full of life, this unique son, this God-engendered, had received a spherical body, the most perfect of all; he was subject to circular movement, the simplest of all, the most suitable to his shape. The Supreme Being surveyed his work with complaisance, and having compared it with the model which He followed in his operations, He recognised with pleasure that the principal traits of the original repeated themselves in the copy. He did not grant him eternity for these two worlds could not have the same perfections. He made time, the mobile image of immobile eternity, which measures the duration of the sensible world as eternity measures that of the intellectual world, and for that He left traces of his presence and his movements. The Supreme Being kindled the sun and cast him with the other planets into the vast solitude of the airs. It is from there that this heavenly body floods the sky with its light.

The contriver of all things then addressed His commandment to the spirits to whom he had entrusted the administration of the heavenly bodies.

"Gods, who owe your birth to Me, listen to My sovereign commands. You do not have the right to immortality; but you participate in it by the power of My will, more powerful than the bonds which unite the parts of which you are composed. It remains for the perfection of all this to fill with inhabitants the seas, the earth, and the airs. If they should owe the day to Me immediately, escape the empire of death, they would become equal to the gods themselves. I thus lay on you the care of producing them. Agents of My power, unite to these perishable bodies the favor of immortality which you have received from My hand. Mold in particular those beings who command other animals and who are submissive to you; who are born by your orders; who increase by your good deeds, and who after their death are reunited with you and participate in your happiness."

He spoke, and suddenly, pouring into the basin where he had kneeded the Soul of the World the remainder of this Soul held in reserve, he then fashioned the individual Souls, and joining to those of men a small portion of the Divine Essence, he attached to them irrevocable destinies. Finally, having appointed to the inferior gods the successive reclothement of mortal bodies to provide for and control their needs, the Supreme Being re-entered into eternal rest. The inferior gods were obliged to employ the same means in developing us and thus the maladies of the body and the even more dangerous ones of the soul. All that is good in the universe in general and in man in particular derives from the Supreme God; all that is defective comes from the vices inherent in matter.

"The earth and the heavens are populated, my dear son, with Spirits to whom the Supreme Being has confided the administration of the Universe; He has distributed them everywhere nature appears to be animated but principally in those regions which stretch around and above us from the earth up to the sphere of the Moon. It is there where an immense authority is exercised, they dispensing life and death, the good and the bad, light and darkness.

"Each nation, each individual finds in these invisible representatives an ardent friend to protect him, an enemy no less ardent to pursue him. They are clothed in an aerial body; their essence holds the middle between Divine Nature and nature; they surpass us in intelligence; some of them are subject to our passions, mostly in the changes which pass them on to a superior rank. Because of their innumerable multitude, spirits are divided into four classes: the first of perfect beings whom the common herd adore and who reside in the stars; the second, those of the spirits properly called and of whom I conversed with you; the third, those beings less perfect who however, render great service to humanity; the fourth, those of our souls, after they have been separated from the bodies which they inhabited. We may discern from the first three the honors which will one day become part of our nature if we cultivate exclusively wisdom and virtue.

"To render you more sensible of that which I have put forward to you relative to the spirits, I will give you an account of what befell me with those who are submissive to me. Know also that they only communicate to souls after a long time of preparation in meditation and prayer. The dominion which I have obtained over my spirit is the result of my constancy in the practice of the virtues. In the beginning I saw him only rarely; one day yielding to my repeated entreaties he transported me to the realm of the spirits. Listen, my son, to the story of my voyage.

'The moment of departure having arrived, I felt my soul detatch itself from the bonds which attached it to the body, and I found myself in the middle of a new world of animated substances, good or malignant, blithe or sad, prudent or careless. We followed them for some time, and I thought I recognized some who were directing the interests of nations and those of individuals, the researches of sages and the opinions of the multitude.

"Soon a woman of gigantic stature extended her black veils over the vault of the skies; and having descended slowly to earth, she gave her orders to the cortege which had accompanied her. We glided into several houses. Sleep and its ministers scattered poppies with full hands; and while silence and peace spread gently around virtuous men, remorses and frightful spectres shook the beds of the wicked with violence.

"'Dawn and the hours open the barriers of the day,' my guide said to me. 'It is time to rise into the air.

See the tutelary spirits of Egypt soaring over the different towns and regions which the Nile irrigates. They dispel as much as possible the evils with which they are menaced; nevertheless, their countryside will be devastated because the spirits enveloped in dark clouds are advancing and thundering against us; he then announced to me the arrival of the army of which you formed a part because he had knowledge of its comming.

'Observe now these assiduous agents, who, with a flight as rapid and as restless as the swallow, skim over the earth and cast piercing looks on all sides for greed and avidity; these are the inspectors of human affairs. Some spread their sweet influence over the mortals whom they protect; others launch the relentless Nemesis against grave transgressions. See these mediators, these expounders who rise and descend without cease; they carry your prayers and your offerings to the gods; they bring back to us happy or distressing dreams and the secrets of the future which are then revealed to you by the mouth of the oracles.'

"Oh my protector!" I cried suddenly, "here are beings which in their stature and sinister appearance inspire terror; they come to us.

"'Flee,' he said to me, 'they are unhappy, the good fortune of others irritates them, and they spare only those who pass their life in sufferings and in tears.'

"Escaping from their fury, we found objects no less afflicting. Discord, the detestable and eternal source of dissentions which torment men, marched proudly above their heads and whispered outrage and vengeance into their hearts. With timid steps and lowered eyes, the prayers trailed on their steps and endeavoured to recall everywhere the calm they had showed themselves. Glory was pursued by envy who tore her own sides; truth by impos re who changed its face from moment to moment; each virtue by several vices which carried snares or knives.

"Fortune appeared suddenly. My guide said to me, 'You can speak with her.' I felicitated her on the gifts which she distributed to mortals. She told me in a serious tone that she did not give but took a great interest. While uttering these words, she soaked the flowers and fruits which she held in one hand in a poisoned cup which she held in the other.

"Then passed near us two powerful spirits who left long trails of light after them. The one was war and the other wisdom.

"My guide told me two armies were approaching each other and were on the point of coming to blows. Wisdom would place herself near the general whose cause was just and he would be the victor because worth must triumph.

"'Let us leave these unhappy spheres,' said my spirit. We leapt the limits of the sphere of darkness and death with the speed of lightning and of thought. We then shot above the sphere of the Moon, and we reached the regions lit by eternal day. 'Let us stop for an instant,' said my guide. 'Cast your eyes over the magnificent spectacle which surrounds you; listen to the divine harmony which is produced by the regular movement of the celestial bodies; look how to each planet, each star, is attached a spirit which directs its course. These heavenly bodies are populated by sublime intelligences of a nature superior to ours.

'With my eyes fixed on the sun, I contemplated with ravishment the spirit who with a vigorous arm pushes this scintillating globe on the course which he has decreed. I watched him cast aside with fury the souls who endeavoured to plunge into the boiling surges of this sphere to purify themselves although they were not worthy of this blessing. Touched by their misfortune, I begged my conductor to take me away from this sight and to lead me into the distance towards an enclosure where one could escape the rays of light which were too brilliant. I hoped to catch a glimpse of the Sovereign of the

Universe surrounded by the assistants of His throne and of those pure beings who our philosophers call numbers, eternal ideas or spirits of the mortals. My spirit told me that the Sovereign inhabits regions inaccessable to humans, that we should offer him our homage and descend to earth.

"Hardly had he spoken when we found ourselves in the same place from whence we had made our departure. He said to me, 'I have let you become acquainted with that which no mortal has ever been permitted to glimpse. From this moment it is no longer forbidden to me to hide anything from you.' And he unveiled to me all the mysteries in which I will let you participate. To convince you of the truth of all that I have given out to you, you will see my spirit, who will become yours since I have adopted you as my son. He will see in you another me '

He pronounced these two words: Koux, Ompax. In that instant I saw appear a young man of the most beautiful stature; the remainder of his person shone with all the charms, and on the summit of his head shone a flame of which my eyes could not sustain the brilliance. He said smiling at the old man: Oles, Nothos, Perius. The old man took his hand and answered: Solathas, Zanteur, Dinanteur. The spirit took his place by his side.

The old man noticed that the spirit's light dazzled my eyes. "When you have been initiated into the mysteries of wisdom, you will be able to contemplate this fire without danger and even to stand the rays of the sun. Let us begin the initiation, let us stand."

I executed this order which he had given as did the spirit. He placed his hand on my head and said:

"Sina, Misas, Tanaim, Orsel, Misanthos." A voice which came from the cavern wherein were the coffers containing all the precious stones gave this answer:

"Torzas, Elicanthus, Orbitau ." Hardly had the last word been pronounced than we found ourselves in the most profound darkness. The fire which shone on the head of the spirit had also disappeared.

"Be without dread or fear," the old man said.

"My father, am I not with you?"

"Your answer pleases me, it proclaims confidence. You will now test the effects of it." He then said: "Thomatos, Benasser, Elianter." Everything was then lit up but by a seemingly dark light, and I saw enter several individuals who took up positions around the room. "Here are all the spirits who will be subservient to you; I will proclaim them to you." He took me by the hand and conducted me around the room. He stopped in front of every spirit and said to me, "Repeat with me: Litau, Izer, Osnas." I obeyed and each spirit bowed saying, "Nanther." There were thirty-three. When we had reached the last one, he told me to return to the place which I had occupied. Then he took a wand six feet in length having at one end the head of a serpent and at the other the tail. On the wand were plates of gold the same as the head and tail on which were engraved the characters as illustrated in Figure 1.

Figure of the Wand stained with blood of the lamb.

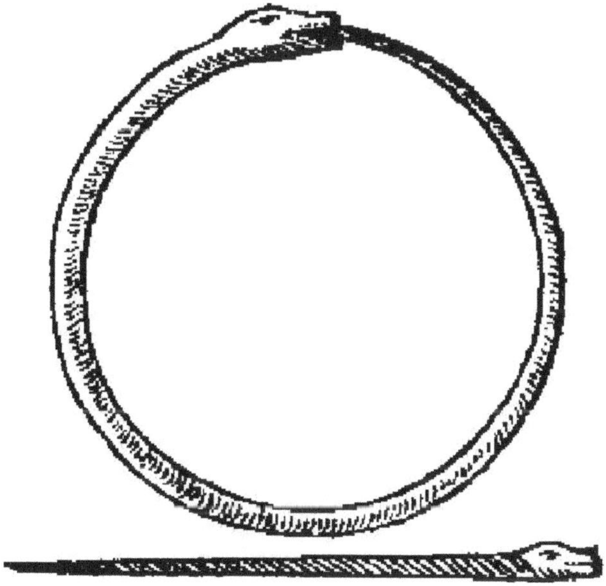

These characters should be written on the wand with India ink.

He formed a circle by uniting each end by a golden chain which he passed through two links; he put it on the ground and placed himself in the center.

"What do you wish to see at this moment, my son?" he asked me.

"The plain on which you found me at the point of death from pain and want," I answered.

He raised his hands toward heaven and said, "Soutram, Ubarsinens." Immediately the spirits approached me and taking me in their arms, they lifted me, and I found myself transported to the foot of the Pyramid. I saw a multitude of Arabs on horseback who were surveying it. Although I had not noticed him, the old man was near me enjoying my astonishment. "You see, my son, how all the spirits are submissive to you, how they will obey you and await your orders. Do you wish to return to the place which you left or to soar for some time in the middle of the aerial parts? Do you know that you can see all that is happening around you and that you are visible only to the Great Being who wishes to accord you wisdom and to those who accompany you?"

I testified to the desire to survey the immensity.

"Pronounce Saram while extending your arms towards the east, and you will be satisfied." I uttered this word and made the indicated sign. The spirits lifted me up as well as the old man. We approached the clouds, and the vast horizon opened to my enchanted eyes. The old man once again said to me: "You see I have not made vain promises, you will have the same success in all your undertakings, but let us return to the Pyramid. The spirits await us, and we will continue our workings." He said "Rabiam," and very soon we re-entered the abode of the old man.

When we were seated, the spirits disappeared, only the first one remaining with us.

All the insignia were changed, and a very intense light illuminated the vault. He then formed the second Magic Circle.

No. 2

Placing himself therein, the old man said to me: "Go near your spirit. I give you permission for I know that you have a pure heart, that you have never been guilty of any action which would make you blush. If that were not the case, you would be struck down dead on entering this circle. Go, my son." I followed his instructions. He opened the casket where all the rings were to be found, and drew out that one shown in Figure 3 as well as the talisman which he placed in my hands.

No. 3

"This one will serve to conjur the celestial and infernal powers. Put the ring on your finger and the talisman over your heart, then pronounce the following words: Siras, Etar, Besanar, and you will perceive the effects."

Hardly had these words come from my mouth than I saw a multitude of spirits and figures of different shapes. The spirit who was at my side said to me: "Command and order and your desires will be satisfied." The old man added, "My son, the sky and the hells are at your orders. I think that at this moment you are not in want of anything; therefore, if you believe me, put off until later proving the Intelligence and activity of these spirits. To make them disappear, remove the ring from your finger and the talisman from the place which it occupies, and they will return to their sphere." I did that which he ordered me to do, and they all went like a dream.

"There remain many things for me to teach you to make you at ease with these rings and talismans. This instruction will be the object of very important work which we shall do together with the help of our spirit.

"Let us follow the course of our experiences. Stay where you are." He gave me another ring and talisman (Figure No. 4).

No. 4

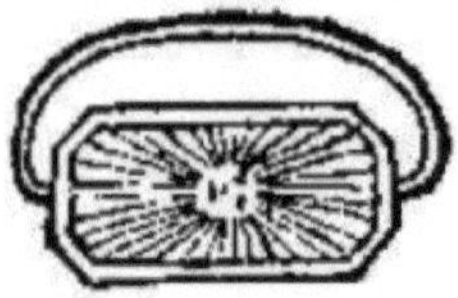

Thesechar actersshouldb eengr avedontheinsideofthering

"These two precious objects, my son, are destined to make you loved by the most beautiful portion of the human race. There is not a woman who would not be happy to please you and who would not employ all possible means to be successful at it. Do you wish the most beautiful odalisque of the Grand Caliph should be brought before you in an instant? Put the ring on the second finger of your left hand, press the talisman against your lips, and say tenderly in a whisper: o Nades, Suradis, Manier." Suddenly a spirit with rose-coloured wings appeared; he placed himself on his knees before me. "He awaits your orders," the old man said. "Say to him: Sader, Prostas, Solaster." I repeated these words, and the spirit vanished. "He is going to traverse an immense space with the rapidity of thought, and the most beautiful forms will appear before your eyes and will serve as a model to paint those houris which our Divine Prophet promises to his faithful servants. O my son, how blessed you are; not every mortal obtains from the Great Spirit such favours as I can see by the speed with which your wishes are executed."

He had finished speaking when the spirit with the rose-coloured wings arrived carrying in his arms a woman enveloped in a large white veil. She seemed to be asleep, and he placed her gently on a couch which appeared near me. He raised the veil which hid her. Never had anything so beautiful been offered to my eyes; she was Venus with all the charms of innocence. She sighed and opened the most beautiful eyes in the world which came to rest on meo In a most harmonious voice she uttered a cry of surprise saying, "It is he." The old man told me to approach the beauty, place a knee on the ground, for it is thus that one should speak to her, and to take her hand. I obeyed, and the divinity to whom I addressed my homage said to me: "I have seen thee in a dream, and the reality thereof makes thee more dear to my heart. I prefer you to the Sultan who for a long time has fatigued me with his homage." "That is enough," said the old man, and he said forcefully, "Mammes Laher." Four slaves appeared to remove the couch and she who had made such a vivid impression on my heart. The old man noticed my emotion and the pain which resulted from her departure. He said to me, "You will see her again. Understand that in order to possess wisdom, it is necessary to know how to resist the allurements of voluptuousness."

His words made me come to myself, and I said to him, "Pardon, my father, but you have seen her, that is my excuse."

I replaced the ring and the talisman in the casket, and he gave me that which is illustrated in Figure No. 5.

No. 5

Thesechar actersshouldb eengr avedontheinsideofthering

"This talisman and this ring are not less valuable.

They will enable you to discover all the treasures which exist and to ensure you the possession of them.

Place the ring on the second finger of your right hand, enclose the talisman with the thumb and little finger of your left hand, and say,Onaim, Perantes,Rasonastos. "

I repeated these three words, and seven spirits of a bronze colour appeared, each carrying a large hide bag which they emptied at my feet. They contained gold coins which rolled in the middle of the hail where we were. I had not noticed that one of the spirits had on his shoulder a black bird, its head covered with a kind of hood.

"It is this bird," the old man said to me, "who has made them find all this treasure. Do not think that these are some of what you have seen here. You can assure yourself of this."

I replied, "You are for me the truth itself. My father! Do you believe that I would insult you by doubting?"

He made a sign, and the spirits replaced the gold in the bags and disappeared.

"You see, my son, what the virtues of these talismans and rings are. When you know them all, you will be able, without my aid, to perform such miracles as you judge proper. Replace in the casket those of which you have made proof, and take this one (Figure No. 6).

No. 6

Thesechar actersshouldb eengr avedontheinsideofthering

"They will enable you to discover the most hidden secrets; you will be able to penetrate everywhere without being seen, and not a single word in the universe can be uttered without it coming to your ears, whether you wish to listen to it yourself or to have it brought back to us by your agents when you order them to do so. To prove it to you, repeat these words and place the talisman near your ear while you hold the ring tightly in your left hand: Nitrae, Radou,Sunandam. " I distinctly heard a voice which said to me:

"The Grand Mogul has decided in his private council that he must declare war on the Emperor of China."

Another voice said to me: "All is rumour in Constantinople. Last night the Sultana was carried off, and the Grand Sultan is in despair. He has had all the eunuchs thrown into the sea after having had them beheaded."

"Oh Heavens! What mischief I have done without wishing it," I cried in pain.

"Well, my son," the old man said, "it is a lesson for you to learn— not to be enslaved by your passions and to know how to curb them. This is enough for today, tomorrow we will continue."

The next day we followed the course of our mysterious operations. The spirit had not left us. "You see, my son," said the old man, "that everything becomes easy with confidence and a pure soul without stain." He opened the casket and took from it the talisman and ring (Figure No. 7).

No. 7

Thesemagicalchar actersshouldb eengr avedontheinsideof thering

When he had placed them in my hands, he pronounced two words, which I will teach you. "Place this ring on the little finger of your left hand and the talisman to your right ear, and the most discreet man will divulge to you his most hidden thoughts. Here are the two words: Noctar, Raiban, and if you add a third word, which is Biranther, your greatest enemies will not be able to prevent themselves from loudly publishing their projects against you. In order to convince you, I am going to have appear before you one of the Beys of Cairo, and he will impart to you all of his schemes against the French." He then said "Nocdar," to the spirit who then vanished like lightening. A quarter of an hour after he returned with the Bey who said: "We have made a treaty of alliance with the English, and the armistice concluded with the French will be broken without warning." He disappeared with the spirit after the old man had said:

"Zelander. The Mufti of the Grand Mosque will appear before your eyes and show you a manuscript of a work which he has composed and which he has refused to show to his best friends, even the Grand Visir." I did that which has previously been indicated, and very soon the Mufti appeared and placing his manuscript on the table, he said to me: "Tonas, Zugar," which means in the language of the magi: read and believe. The old man looked at him affectionately; he gave him his hand pronounced with sweetness and expression, o Solem. The Mufti, after bowing, disappeared.

"Return the talisman and the ring to me," the old man said, "and take this." (Figure No. 8)

No. 8

Characterstob eengr avedontheinsideofthering

"It will serve to activate as many spirits as you wish to undertake or to stop operations which would be contrary to you. The magic words are: Zorami, Zaitux, Elastot. We will not at this moment make any experiments; tomorrow we will go to the shores of the Nile and we will have constructed a bridge of a single arch on which we shall pass to the other side of the river.

"Here is the next talisman and its ring (Figure No. 9).

No. 9

Thesechar actersshouldb eengr avedontheinsideofthering

They have the property of destroying everything, of commanding the elements, of calling down the thunder, hail, the stars, earthquakes, hurricanes, water spouts on land and sea, and of preserving our friends from all accidents. Here are the words which one must pronounce (the numbers indicate each thing that you wish to operate): first, you pronounce: Ditau, Hurandos; second, Ridas,

Talimol; third, Atrosis, Narpida; fourth, Uusur, Itar; fifth, Hispen, Tromador; sixth,Paranthes, Histanos.

"The talisman and the ring (Figure No. 10) will make you invisible to all eyes, even those of the spirits. Only the Great Being could be witness to your steps and your actions. You will penetrate everywhere into the bosom of the seas, into the bowels of the earth, you can likewise survey the airs, and no action of men can be hidden from you. Say only: Benatir, Cararkau, Dedos, Etinarmi."

No. 10

Characterstob eengr avedontheinsideofthering

I repeated these four words, and through the walls of the Pyramid I saw two Arabs who were on the plain and who were profiting by the obscurity to ransack a tomb where they hoped to find something of value. "You will be able, when you wish, to prove the other things which I will have taught you, it will only be necessary to place the ring successively on the different fingers of the right hand.

"The talisman and ring (Figure No. 11) will serve to transport you into whatever part of the world you judge appropriate without running any danger. Say merely these words: Raditus, Polastrien, Terpandu, Ostrata, Pericatur, Ermas. But I hope that you will not make use of these means to leave me without my consent. Promise it to me." "My father, I swear to it."

No. 11

Characterstob eengr avedontheinsideofthering

"With the talisman and the ring (Figure No. 12) you will be able to open all locks, no matter what secrets have been employed to shut them; you will not need a key. Simply by touching them with the ring and pronouncing these three words: Saritap,

Pernisox, Ottarim, they will open of themselves without difficulty. Make proof of this on the spot, my son," the old man told me. "Close the casket which you see on that table." I did this, and after having assured myself that nothing could open it but the key, I touched it with the ring and pronounced the magic words, and it opened of its own accord. "It will be the same," added the old man, "with all the doors of prisons, fortified castles, where they might lock you up.

No. 12

Characterstob eengr avedontheinsideofthering

"With the talisman and ring (Figure No. 13), you will be able to see what takes place in all houses without being obliged to enter them; you will be able to read the thoughts of everyone whom you approach and with whom you find yourself, and you will be able to render them service or do them injury as you wish. It will be sufficient to place the talisman on your head and then to blow on the ring saying: o Tarot, Nizael, Estarnas, Tantarez these words are for knowing the thoughts of people.

"In order to render service to those who deserve it, you say: Nista, Saper, Visnos, and they will immediately enjoy all sorts of prosperities.

"To punish the wicked and your enemies, you will say: Xatros, Nifer, Roxas, Rortos, and they will at once suffer punishment and frightful torment. What you have already seen should prove to you that I have advanced nothing which cannot be realised; therefore it is useless to make proof thereof.

No. 13

Characters to be engraved on the inside of the ring

"The talisman and the ring (Figure No. 14) will serve you to destroy all the projects which could be made against you, and if any spirit wished to oppose your wishes, you could force him to submit to you.

Place the talisman on a table under your left hand and with the ring on the second finger of the right hand, you say in a bass voice, while inclining your head:

Senapos, Terfita, Estamos, Perfiter, Notarin.

No. 14

Characterstob eengr avedontheinsideofthering

"The talisman and ring (Figure No. 15) have a property as extraordinary as agreeable; they will give you all the virtues, all the talents, and the inclination to do good by changing all substances which are of a bad quality and rendering them excellent. For the first object, while elevating the talisman and with the ring placed on the first joint of the third finger of the left hand, it is sufficient to pronounce these words:T uran, Estonos, Fuza.

"For the second operation you say: Vazotas, Testanar, and you will see operate the wonder which I have proclaimed to you.

No. 15

Characterstob eengr avedontheinsideofthering

"The talisman and the ring (Figure No. 16) will assist you to know all the minerals and vegetables, their virtues and properties, and you will possess the universal medicine. There is no illness that you will not be able to cure and no cure that you will undertake without success. Aesculapius and Hippocrates will only be novices compared to you. You pronounce only these words: Reterrem, Salibat, Cratares, Hisater, and when you are near a sick person you will carry thet talisman on the stomach and the ring with a St. Andrew's Cross around your neck on a ribbon the colour of fire.

No. 16

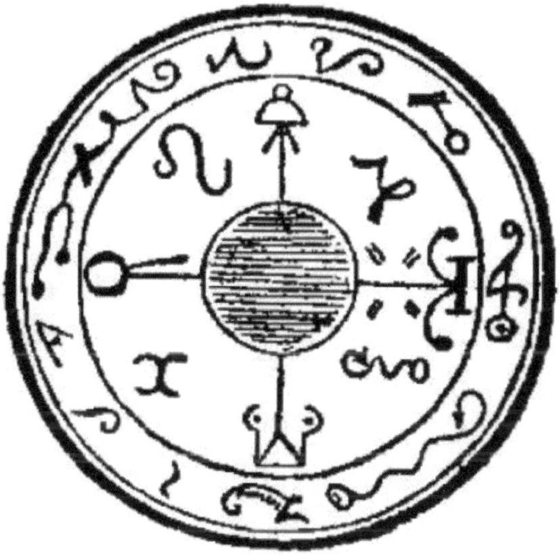

Characterstob eengr avedontheinsideofthering

"The talisman and the ring (Figure No. 17) will keep you safe in the midst of the most ferocious animals, to subdue them to your will, to know by their different cries what they want as they have a language among themselves. Mad animals will keep at a distance from you, and you will make them perish forthwith by pronouncing the words which I am going to indicate to you.

"For the first operation it is sufficient to say: Hocatos, Imorad, Surater, Markila. For the second:T rumantrem, Ricona, Estupit, Oxa.

No. 17

Characterstob eengr avedontheinsideofthering

"The talisman and ring (Figure No. 18) will enable you to know the good or bad intentions of all the individuals whom you will meet to guarantee you of it and to impress on their face a mark which will be noticed by everyone. It is sufficient to pronounce these mysterious words, while placing the talisman on your heart and the ring on the little finger of your right hand. You will then say: Crostes, Furinot, Katipa,Garinos.

No. 18

Characterstob eengr avedontheinsideofthering

"The talisman and the ring (Figure No. 19) will give you all talents and a profound understanding of all the arts so that you can perform with as much brilliance as the greatest masters and foremost artists. It is sufficient to carry the talisman and the ring in a manner you judge suitable while pronouncing these seven words: Ritas, Onalun, Tersorit, Ombas, Serpitas, Quitathar, Zamarath while adding afterwards the name of the art or the talent which you wish to possess.

No. 19

"The talisman and the ring (Figure No. 20) will help you to win at lotteries and to make certain when playing a game that you will obtain the fortune of your adversaries. You will place the talisman on your left arm, adjusting it with a white ribbon, and the ring on the little finger of your right hand; then you will say these words: Rokes for a selection, Pilatus for a combination of two numbers, Zotas for dice, Tulitas for four winning numbers, Xatanitos for five winning numbers. Be sure to pronounce all the words when you are on a quine, and for a card game you will pronounce them each time the cards are shuffled, if it is you or your partner, and before commencing you will touch your left arm on the spot where the talisman is to be found with your right hand, and you will kiss your ring. All this must be done without drawing the attention of your adversary.

No. 20

Characterstob eengr avedontheinsideofthering

"The talisman and the ring (Figure No. 21) will enable you to direct all the infernal powers against your enemies or against those who would injure your friends. You will carry it in a manner which you consider suitable and pronounce merely these three words:Osthariman, Visantip aros, Noctatur.

No. 21

Characterstob eengr avedontheinsideofthering

"The talisman and the ring (Figure No. 22) will serve you to recognise what the infernal powers wish to undertake, and you can abort all their projects by placing the talisman on your chest and the ring on the first joint of the little finger of the left hand. You pronounce these words: Actatos, Catipta, Bejouran, Itapan, Marnutus.

No. 22

Characterstob eengr avedontheinsideofthering

Composition of the Talismans and the Rings.

"As it is possible that you have not had the means of making talismans and rings similar to mine," the old man said to me, "you will make them up in the manner which I will indicate. Know that the rings are of bronzed steel with the characters engraved thereon. The talismans should be made of silk cloth in the dimensions of the figures.

No. 1. White satin embroidered in gold.

No. 2. Red satin embroidered in silver.

No. 3. Sky-blue satin embroidered in silver.

No. 4. Black satin embroidered in silver.

No. 5. Green satin embroidered in gold.

No. 6. Violet satin embroidered in silver.

No. 7. Golden-yellow satin embroidered in gold.

No. 8. Lilac satin with shaded silk.

No. 9. Poppy-red satin embroidered in silver.

No. 10. Yellow satin embroidered in black silk.

No. 11. Puce satin embroidered in gold.

No. 12. Dark blue satin embroidered in silver.

No. 13. Pale grey satin embroidered in gold.

No. 14. Rose satin embroidered in silver.

No. 15. Golden-yellow satin embroidered in silver.

No. 16. Orange satin embroidered in silver.

No. 17. Dark green satin embroidered in gold.

No. 18. Black satin embroidered in gold.

No. 19. White satin embroidered in black silk.

No. 20. Cherry satin embroidered in silver.

No. 21. Grey-White satin, shaded.

No. 22. Red satin, embroidered in the middle with gold, the border in silver, and the signs in black and white silk.

The old man, after having given me this information, replaced all the talismans and rings in the casket. The spirit who was at my side closed it arid gave him the key. The old man said to me: "All the wonders which have been performed in front of You, my dear son, ought not to leave any doubt of the Power and virtue of these talismans and rings. If you have not experienced any obstacle in your enterprises, it is because your heart is pure, that your soul is without stain, and that virtue, probity, and honour will always be dear to you. A man who had the least reproach to make to himself, who had destroyed the good of others, or who had only the intention of so doing, would not be able to participate in our mysteries. In vain would he have in his possession all that you see, our magical language known to him. The celestial powers—aerial, infernal, terrestrial, and those of the oceans and fire—would rebel against him. All that he wished to undertake would turn to his shame and his confusion, and at each invocation which he might make, the powers that he implored for help and intervention would answer him: Renounce thy projects. Thou art guilty. Before commanding us, purify thyself, expiate thy faults.

"If after these emanations he continued to conjure the powers, he would finish by being punished and would without fail lose his life. Remember then, my dear son, that all is possible with virtue and that not one fault will remain unpunished. There are still two prayers which you must be careful to recite before and after each conjuration that you wish to do; here they are:

First Prayer.

The Celestial Fire above is an incorruptable flame, always scintillating, the source of life, fountain of all the Beings, and principle of all things. This flame produces all and nothing perishes except which it consumes: it makes itself known by it-self. This fire cannot be contained in any place; it is without body or matter. It encompasses the skies, and from it emanates a little spark which makes all fire of the Sun, of the Moon, and the Stars. That is what I know of God: do not try to know more because that is beyond you, such judge as thou art. Moreover, know that the unjust or wicked man can-not hide himself in front of God; no address or any excuse can disguise anything from his piercing eyes. All is clear to God: God is everywhere.

Second Prayer.

There is in God as immense profundity of flame; the heart ought not, however, to fear to touch or to be touched by this adorable fire; it will not be consumed by this sweet fire, whose tranquil and perishable heat makes the union, harmony, and duration of the world. Nothing exists except by this fire which is God. No one has engendered it; it is without mother, it knows all, and no one is able to know anything of it. It is immovable in its projects and its name is ineffable. Here then is that which is God; because for us, who are his messengers, we are but a small part of God.

"You see, my son, that all the instructions that I give you have as a basis the respect which one owes to God, Who is the principle of all things and Whose ineffable and limitless goodness fills us to the brim each day with all His goodness, when we render ourselves worthy of it by our respect and our submission to His will and His immutable decree."

The old man after these short reflections said to me: "You have no doubt noticed, my son, that I have spoken to you about the birds to whom I was going to give food, and you have seen spirits who had one with them; when the pieces of gold were deposited at your feet, it was these birds who enabled them to discover it by their instinct and by the magical and cabalistic words which one pronounced. To procure these birds there are difficulties without number that one must conquer, and the profane, those who are not initiated into our mysteries, make useless efforts to obtain them. It is of the marvelous Black Hen that I am going to converse with you. The great Oromasis, father of Zoroaster, was the first who possessed one; it is from him that I possess the secret of calling them into existence, and here is the manuscript in which is contained the manner of hatching these birds who are as rare as precious." He opened for me at the same time this manuscript whose cover was a thin plate of gold covered with diamonds, rubies, topazes and sapphires whose brilliance it was impossible to bear. The paper was of a dazzling whiteness, and the hieroglyphic characters were traced by hand in rose-coloured ink.

"I will teach YOU to read in this book as I can," he said to me, "but let us occupy ourselves with the way to hatch the Black Hen and to procure the eggs which she will come forth." He took several pieces of aromatic woods such as aloes, cedar, or lemon, laurel, some root of Iris, and some roses whose leaves had been dried in the sun. (Translators note: the author distinctly states leaves, not petals.) He put the lot in a chafing-dish of gold. poured on top thereof balsamic oil of the purest essence, transparent gum, and having pronounced the words: Athas, Solinam, Erminatos, Pasaim, the sun-light penetrated the vault. He placed a glass on the chafing-dish. At the same moment that the sun's struck the glass, the perfumes and pieces of odorous wood which were in the dish burst into flame, the glass liquified, and an agreeable odor was diffused in the vault. Very soon nothing was left but cinders. The old man, who had not ceased to watch with the greatest attention, took a golden egg which been in a black velvet bag and which I had not noticed. He opened this egg, closed the burning cinders therein, and placed it then on a black cushion. He covered it with a faceted rock-crystal bell; then, raising his eyes and his arms toward the vault, he cried: oSanataper, Ismai, Nontapilus, Ertivaler, Canopistus. The sun seemed to dart its rays on this bell with still greater force and violence.

The bell became the colour of fire, the golden egg disappeared before my eyes, a thin vapour rose in the air, and I saw a little black pullet which stirred, got to its feet and clucked faintly. The old man extended one of his fingers to it, and it placed itself thereon. He then pronounced these two words: Binusas, Testipas, and the winged creature glided onto his breast.

There," said the old man, "is the manner of procuring a Black Hen. In a few days it will be of ordinary size, and I will instruct it in front of you. You will see the instinct of this animal to discover the most hidden treasures and that the smallest particle of gold cannot escape it. Let us give thanks to the Great Being who has permitted us to penetrate these mysteries and to perform such prodigies and marvels. We will say together the two prayers recounted further back." After having fulfilled this duty, he said to me, "My son, this is enough. We will take a little rest." The sun had shone on us for some time. It disappeared, and its light was replaced by that of several chandeliers. The spirit, who had not left us, took a lyre, and accompanying himself he sang in the language of the magicians of the Eternal Power and the marvels of nature.

The old man listened with attention to the accents of the spirit. For myself I was enchanted, and he smiled in observing me. "This is enough," he said to the spirit. "Before delivering ourselves to rest, I wish to show you the means of having a Black Hen without having recourse to those which I have used, for it would be difficult to obtain the perfumes and the other materials which I placed in the chaffing-dish if others than you or I wished to perform this great work. But if someday you find someone who is worthy of being initiated, here is the means which you should employ. Take an egg which you will expose at noon to the gleams of the sun, observing that it has not the least stain. Then you choose a hen as black as possible; if it has any feathers of another colour, you will pull them out. You will cover its head with a hood of black material in such a manner that it can-not distinguish anything. You will allow it the use of it's beak. Enclose it in a box lined also with black material, big enough to contain it, and place that in a room where daylight cannot penetrate. Be careful to bring it food only at night. When all these indispensible precautions have been taken, you will give it the egg to sit on, taking care that it is not disturbed by any noise. It all depends on the blackness of this hen, its imagination will be impressed with it, and at the proper time you will see hatched a hen which is completely black. But I repeat to you, is necessary that those who perform this shall be worthy by their wisdom and virtue to participate in these sacred and divine mysteries. For, if we are not able to read the hearts of men, it is not the same with the Great Spirit; all is known to him and he penetrates our most secret intentions and our most hidden thoughts. It is after that that He accords or refuses to us His favours and His gifts.

"Our sitting has been so long," he added, "that We must take some food before delivering ourselves to rest." He clapped his hands three times, and the Slaves, the spirits who had previously appeared, offered themselves again to my attention, and in an instant we had all the viands that could satisfy taste aroma, and the eyes. The meal was very gay; the old man annimated it by his sallies. The spirit was also of the party. I was as inspired, and I joined the conversation. At last sleep weighed down our eyes, and we left the table to taste its sweetness.

The most agreeable dreams lulled me with their cheerful images, and when I awoke daylight lit up our abode. I did not see the old man or the spirit. I thought that they had gone out, and I abandoned myself to my reflections. The present assures me of the future, nothing could make me anxious. If fortune gives happiness, I said to myself, who will be happier than I. I cannot see any wish which will not be accomplished at once; my lot would be envied if it were known by the remainder of men. I want to be able to return to my country soon. As I followed up this idea, I heard a slight noise and saw the old man enter followed by the spirit. They approached me, both took me by the hand, and I left my bed of rest at once.

'You have rested well, my dear son," the old man said. "During your sleep I went out with the spirit to visit my birds, and I am going to make you acquainted with their talents. At the same instant he touched a spring which was in the wall, a section opened, and seven black birds which I recognised as hens were brought in in a cage by two black slaves. "These animals have a marvelous instinct for finding gold. You will be the judge." He placed several pieces of gold under the cushions, in the crevices of walls under the folds of his turban, then said to the slaves: Tournabos, Fativos, Almabisos. They opened the cage, uncovered the heads of the birds, and the hens came out and flew immediately in the different places where the gold was hidden. They picked up the pieces in their beaks and deposited them at the feet of the old man. He took these birds one after the other and carressed them. He said to me: "You see how tame they are; we will go out for a while on the plain; I have placed in the sand several pieces of gold. We will release our birds, and soon they will have discovered the treasure." He made a sign to the slaves who reclosed the birds in the cage we departed.

As soon as we had come out of the Pyramid for about five hundred paces onto the plain, he released the birds. They went a few paces; soon it seemed that their instinct indicated to them where the treasure was to be found. They flew in that direction, and all seven of them started scratching. They soon discovered the sacks, and one of them started to cackle; we approached and saw the sacks which the old man had hidden. I could not prevent myself from showing my surprise. "My son, you see that all is possible with the aid of God and his powerful protection." We took the sacks and re-entered the Pyramid.

He had the birds re-enclosed with the same precautions as were taken to let them out. He then said to me: "Let us see what condition my new-born is in." He opened a little box lined with down in which he had enclosed it, and already feathers were beginning to appear. "A few more days," he said, "and it will be able to receive the first lessons. He replaced the box in its place. "Since we have been together," said the old man, "we have not gone out; we will make a little excursion into the country and wear the costume of the locality." The spirit covered his head with a turban and dressed completely like a Turk. I did the same, and we prepared to depart. Before leaving I saw the old man take a talisman and a ring. I remarked on it, and he told me that perhaps it might be necessary for us and that precaution was the mother of security. We then went our way and walked quietly for some time. The old man spoke to us of the changes which took place in the world from time to time, of the revolution of the stars and the planets.

He seemed to give notice to us and to fore-shadow things which would follow. All of a sudden a horde of Arabs pounced upon us with raised swords. The old man looked at them without fright, and he raised his hand; the brigands stopped. He pronounced the words prescribed for the talisman (Figure No. 10) and we became invisible. The astonished Arabs looked on all sides without seeing us. It is impossible to paint a picture of the astonishment of these villains. Their chief appeared astounded. The old man smiled. He pronounced the word Natarter in a loud voice, and they took flight with lightening rapidity. "Be calm," said the old man. "For a long time they will not dare to appear in this territory."

We continued walking for some time. The time passed with an extraordinary rapidity; the conversation of the old man was so varied, so instructive, that it was impossible to listen to him without being charmed by all that he said. "Let us return to our abode." After having pronounced these words, he looked at the sun and cried: "Brilliant star, image of the Divinity, thou who vivifies the earth and gives life to nature, receive my homage; may I ere I leave the earth constantly enjoy thy light."

"What has given birth to these somber ideas," I immediately cried. "Why do you think of leaving earth?"

"Ah, my son! Each day which passes, each that we take leads us towards the tomb. Lucky is the just man who can go to sleep in peace in the care of God to enjoy thereafter the rewards promised to virtue. Also, my son, do you believe that I do not concern myself with my last hour? At my age it is permitted to think of it, and I have always lived in a manner so as to be able to die without fear. I am 270 years old, and I have seen many things pass; I will pass also when my turn comes. And now enough of this matter. I see that I trouble you, and that is not my intention. Let us talk of other things.

"The talisman and ring (Figure No. 20) will furnish you with the means to win at lotteries. I wish also to indicate to you an infallible calculation to obtain the same advantages. It is really very simple. You take a game of piquet composed of thirty-two cards. You shuffle them, cut and extract nineteen cards one after the other commencing with that which is underneath. Take their numbers: know, the ace is 11, the king 4, the queen 3, the knave 2, and the other cards their numerical value. Add up the total. Then add the 30 or 31 days of the month in which you find yourself, your age, the day of your birth, that is to say, the first, second or third or such other day, and a date when you have proved something happy or agreeable: you add all these numbers, you take a third of it, and you place in the lottery the numbers which this addition has given you. You can be certain that these numbers will come out in totality or in part on the different wheels. For instance, if you find the numbers 13, 52, 73, you can take again 31, 25, 37, and the unities. This calculation is infallible. You can convince yourself. The number 30 is priviledged, and it is from this that all is calculated for 3 times 30 makes 90; it is from this that one does not wish to exceed this number in the lottery. It is the same with all games.

"The numbers which have 3 for a root are the most fortunate; odd is all. God, after having created the world and being occupied for six days in establishing the admirable order which exists, rested on the seventh, which is odd. Let us take God as an example and a model in all that we do and we will be assured in all that we undertake. You have noticed, my son, that odd numbers are the basis of all the mysterious operations into which I have initiated you."

We continued our route and arrived at the Pyramid. He opened the door, and we went down. Arriving in the hall, we sat down on a sofa which faced the table on which was the casket of the tasilmans. The old man replaced the one which had served to clear away the Arabs, and we remained in silence for some time.

The old man appeared tired. He reclined on the and soon he was asleep. I cast my eyes on his venerable figure, and I admired his serenity, Calmness spread over all his features. I remarked about this to the spirit who told me: "It is the image of his soul. I have obeyed him for more than a century. You cannot have any idea of his virtue, of his wisdom, of his goodness. His days are numerous, and all are marked by some good deed, of the unhappy he has rescued without their ever knowing who the being was who came to their help. If the eternal Soul who has created all should take the figure of a mortal, it is his which He would borrow. Is not the just man in effect the image of God on earth? Many have taken title, but how many have usurped it and merited little." After having pronounced these words, the spirit got up, knelt on the ground near the old man, and raising his hands and eyes towards heaven, said in a solemn tone which awed me:

"Eternal Spirit, Who hears me and Who reads heart, prolong the life of this virtuous man. Ensure that he adorns by his presence for a long time to come the earth which You enrich with Thy gifts, unless You have reserved for him near Thee a reward worthy of him."

The sentiments with which he expressed these words keenly moved me. Tears wet my eyes, and I fell on my knees as he had.

The old man awoke at this moment, and casting his eyes on us, he said to us with a smile, "What are you doing, my children?" I answered that we were praying to the Great Being to conserve our father for us. "My good friends," answered the old man, "our life has a term set by Providence which we cannot extend: everything begins, everything must end; God alone is eternal. The only thing which can survive us is the memory of our virtues and the good examples which we have set. While like voyagers we can perceive the course of our destiny and what good or evil we have done as we have been more or less the slaves of our passions, happy is he who has been able to command himself and to distinguish the happiness which is praiseworthy from what is not. For myself, I have been happy enough; I made the distinction in the springtime of my life, and in the winter I taste the sweetness. I shall soon return into the bosom of Him who has created me; a dream announced it to me in my sleep. In a few hours my soul will leave its mortal remains and will rise towards the celestial regions."

"Oh heavens! my father," I cried, "what do you announce?"

"What you must await like myself, my dear son but I bless my departure since I have the consolation in dying of leaving my heritage to a man who is deserving, who loves virtue, who practices it, and who will never step aside from it. I will inform you of my last wishes, and you will execute them punctually if you love me and if you are grateful."

"Oh my father!" I cried, "can you doubt it?"

"No, my dear son, I do not doubt at all. Now listen to me. All these treasures, all the jewels enclosed in this subterranean apartment, also the talismans and the rings, the slaves, and the birds which you have seen are yours. To you Odous," he said to the spirit, "I cannot do more than pronounce all my tenderness for one whom I have found worthy to succeed me. Love him, serve him as you would me, and from the Celestial Sphere to which I shall soon arise, I will watch over you." He clapped his hands and all the slaves appeared. "Here is your master," he said to them. "Be obedient to him, I order you." They all came and prostrated themselves at my feet. "Extend your hand over them as a sign of domination," the old man said to me. I obeyed. They arose, and the old man's having made a sign, they disappeared.

He added, "Take the gold urn which you will find in the cabinet on the right and place it on the table. When I no longer exist, place my body in the middle of this chamber. Take the aromatic woods, which you will find near the coffers filled with gold, and surround me with them. After having poured over the pyre the liquid enclosed in the vase suspended from the roof, you will use the talisman with which I formed the egg in which was enclosed the Black Hen. After having pronounced the mysterious words, you will set the funeral-pile on fire to consume my mortal remains. Take the ashes and enclose them in the urn. Conserve them. Men, cherish my memory; I die content. I would have liked to show you the means of instructing the little Black Pullet, but Heaven which knows our projects has not wished it so. Odous will teach you; he also knows this secret. I feel my soul ready to fly away. Come, my dear son, dry your tears so that I can press you once again to my heart. Remember, death is only dreaded by the guilty and the unjust man." I approached him and he gave me a last kiss. "Good-bye, my dear son," he said. "Listen to my last wishes."

While I was still bending over the sofa, he expired. I could not help myself saying, while sobbing, that the death of the just is sweet and worthy of envy. I fell almost unconscious at the feet of my benefactor. Odous brought me back to my senses by observing that we had to obey our father. We then punctually performed that which he had ordered, and soon there remained only the ashes of the most just and most virtuous of men.

I said to Odous, "We will leave this day and make all the necessary arrangements for returning to my country. "I am with you," answered the spirit. "Your wishes are law for me; command and I obey." I had all the slaves brought before me and had them put on French costumes. It sufficed me to have recourse to the talismans. I had all the treasures and the effects which were in the underground vaults transported to the banks of the Nile and provided for the precious urn which I personally kept. Odous found a boat. We went down the river, and very soon we entered the roadstead where a vessel was about to set sail for Marseilles. I boarded with all my people, and soon we were in mid-ocean. The captain of the vessel and the sailors examined us with extreme curiosity. As I spoke all languages at will, they were even more surprised.

Night came and the wind rose. The captain told me that he feared a storm. I told him that his vessel was good and would resist it. That which he foretold arrived; the sea became furious. Fear and despair were on all faces. The pilot could no longer control the ship. Only I, calm and tranquil, seemed unmoved. Provided with the talisman and ring (Figure No. 9) and pronouncing the mysterious words, I seized the tiller and the vessel which, the instant before, was the plaything of the winds and the surrounding waves, sailed forward lightly over the vast bosom of the sea. The whole crew regarded me as a god, even giving me that name. "I am but man," I told them. "My friends, I do not frighten easily, I know the art of navigation, and you see, it is only necessary to be composed to stand the storm at bay."

The rest of our voyage was very happy. We arrived at Marseilles, and we passed through quarantine before stepping ashore. I paid for my passage and that of my followers with a generosity which astonished the captain. I gave a present to each man of the crew, and I departed crowned with their blessings. I stayed for some time at Marseilles.

Having written to the place of my birth, I found that my parents no longer were alive. They had died during my absence leaving me sole heir to their estates which I sold and the proceeds of which were sent to me. I bought a lovely property on the outskirts of Marseilles, the beautiful sky of Provence pleasing me. I improved my house, and I had a delightful stay. The riches I possessed were such that I could obtain at will all that I desired, even to place myself to my satisfaction. I had a few friends to whom I gave advice, who followed it, and who were all astonished at their prosperity. They were ignorant as to the source. I did not share my secrets with anyone.

Inclination has made me write this little volume. If those who procure it know how to profit from it and are worthy of penetrating the mysteries and the secrets it contains, they will gamble with luck reserved for virtue and wisdom. They must not become discouraged. Constant and stubborn work will surmount everything says an ancient proverb. They should thus work, and if success does not crown their efforts, they must lay the blame on themselves. It is because they are not pure and virtuous. The incredulous, the ignorant, and many others whom it is useless to designate will treat me as a fool, a visionary, an importunist. It matters little to me. The truth is there. I do not seek to repel injuries, still less censure. Certain family libraries, which have no other merit than to get hold of what belongs to others, will perhaps make haste to publish a surreptitious edition of this work. This is the only thing which I will punish with a talisman which I am keeping to myself and a ring more curious still. I reserve for myself the decoration the perpetrator with two ears six inches longer than those provided of yore for King Midas who had been well judged. It is a warning which I give in passing to certain editors. You notice that for a sorcerer I do not push my vengeance very far.

And you, for whom I have written this work, you who seek to enlighten yourself, to penetrate, to understand the mysteries and the secrets of nature, work with consistency, persevere, purify yourself to obtain success, the object of your wishes and your desires. Consider that the smallest stain with which your heart and your soul will be contaminated will be an invincible obstacle against success. You will see the harbour without being able to enter and will be shipwrecked at the moment when you believe yourself saved. Watch, pray, hope. Adieu my dear and well loved readers. May you be able to play with all the ease which has become my lot. Amen.

The old man did not indicate to me the method of instructing the Black Pullet which he had hatched, but before expiring, he informed me that Odous would impart the important secret to me. When we were installed in my home in Marseilles, I reminded him of the old man's promise. The Hen was of ordinary size and was eager to satisfy me. It had become so familiar that it hardly ever left me. I took particular care of it during our voyage, and if I have not mentioned this fact, it is because I judged it of little importance. We therefore occupied ourselves with the education of our bird. We placed a piece of gold in the basket where it was in the habit of sleeping and covered its eyes with the hood of which I have already spoken. Two or three days after that preliminary operation, each morning when I took it food to eat, it scratched in its basket, and taking the piece of gold in its beak, it guarded it until I took it.

One can see that the instinct of this bird was as extraordinary as marvelous. Odous said to me, "I have never yet seen as intelligent a one, but also, it is necessary to admit that our good and respected father employed a means to give it birth which was known only to himself and which he had never put into operation in front of me. This proves the tenderness and friendship he had given you. It will be necessary as from tomorrow to hide a piece of gold in the garden. We will carry our Hen to some distance, and we will see if she discovers it." The next morning we did as agreed. I uncovered the head of my bird; it stayed on my knees for some time, looking in different directions. Finally, it jumped lightly to the ground and ran to the foot of a big tree which was opposite us. It started to scratch animatedly. Odous said to me: "I guarantee that there is some treasure hidden at the foot of that tree. Let the Hen carry on." She scratched all the time and to shorten the operation, I took a spade which the gardner had left nearby, and after having scooped out about two feet, I discovered a case about four feet square and surrounded with iron bands. As we did not have the key, I sent Odous to find the talisman (Figure No. 12). He returned promptly and hardly had I attacked the lock with the ring than it opened, and we discovered several sacks filled with gold and silver, plate, diamonds, jewels, and several other precious objects which were valued at 1,500,000 francs. It seemed that these riches had been concealed in this place during the time of the civil troubles, and as the owners died without revealing their secret, nobody had any knowledge of this deposit. I had bought this property from distant relatives. I could not prevent myself, nor could Odous, from admiring the instinct of our Black Hen, but it was equally necessary for it to find the other piece of hidden gold. We advanced a few steps, and she followed us. Soon she went ahead of us and stopped near the place where the gold was hidden. She soon found it and taking it in her beak, she deposited it at my feet. "Charming bird," I cried! "How precious you are to me. You have put me in the place of a better man, the most tender and respected of fathers to me."

Odous said to me: "See if she will listen to the sacred words which must be pronounced every day to the Black Hen to indicate to her that she must look for things." He then articulated certain words, Nozos, Taraim, Ostus. The Hen appeared to pay attention and to understand because she started to scratch near us and found a ruby mounted in a golden ring. "I am going to pronounce three other words which should indicate to her that she should repose near her master." He then said: Seras, Coristan, Abattuzas. The Hen came and placed herself at my feet. Odous added: "All the hens which you possess know these words but it has taken some time to teach them. One must hold them with a ribbon: when pronouncing the first words, one must make them walk; when pronouncing the second, one stops them. As these birds are endowed with a particular instinct, they then do that which one desires."

Having the casket brought in by my slaves, I added the Pullet's findings to those which I already possessed.

I had an elegant pavilion constructed of Cremona marble, and I placed the urn containing the ashes of the old man on a black marble pedestal with a silver plaque which expressed my recognition and regrets. I had cypresses and weeping willows planted, and every day at the rising of the sun, I went, followed by Odous, to visit this pavilion and to pass an hour in support of our good father, remembering the lessons and examples of virtue which he had given me. I will cite several events with great solemnity: that on which he saved my life by taking me into the Pyramid and the anniversary of his death. This day was consecrated to grief and meditation in my house. And once every year all my slaves entered the drove which I had had surrounded with a metal grill so that nobody could enter. Also, the thickness of the bushes and the winding paths which had to be wandered through before arriving at the pavilion prevented the most piercing eye from seeing it. My days passed between work, study, meditation, and walking exercise. I received a few visitors in my home, but nobody had an inkling of that which passed in my private life. To live happily, live concealed, as a Sage said. And this proverb is the rule and foundation of my conduct.

Table des matières